A true story from the Bible

Rowan
with lots of love
from
Granny & Grandpa

Christmas 2022

NOAH
and the
VERY BIG
BOAT

· WRITTEN BY ·
Tim Thornborough

· ILLUSTRATED BY ·
Jennifer Davison

Have you noticed that we say things
over and over again?

Sometimes it's because we don't get an answer the
first time — "Are we nearly there yet?"
Sometimes it's just because it's fun —"The wheels
on the bus go round and round, round and round…"
And sometimes it's to let someone know that we
really, really mean it.

This book repeats lots of things — sometimes
so that we know that it's important, and sometimes
just for fun,

I hope you really really really enjoy reading it!

Noah and the Very Big Boat © The Good Book Company, 2019
Words by Tim Thornborough. Illustrations by Jennifer Davison. Design and art direction by André Parker
thegoodbook.co.uk • thegoodbook.com • thegoodbook.com.au • thegoodbook.co.nz • thegoodbook.co.in
ISBN: 9781784983802. Printed in India

"I am sad, sad, sad," said God
"because everyone is...

BAD
BAD
BAD

God said to Noah, "I'm going to...

SPLASH SPLASH SPLASH

them all away."

But I promise I will keep
you and your family...

SAFE
SAFE
SAFE"

God told Noah to build a Very Big Boat.

CHOP CHOP CHOP CHIP CHIP CHIP

BAM
BAM
BAM

BASH
BASH
BASH

Noah did exactly
what God said.

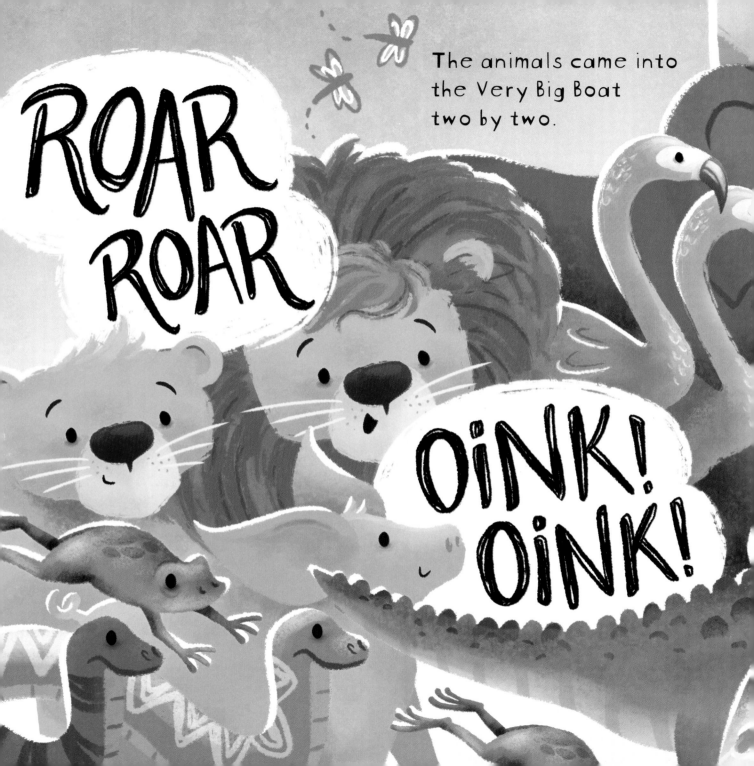

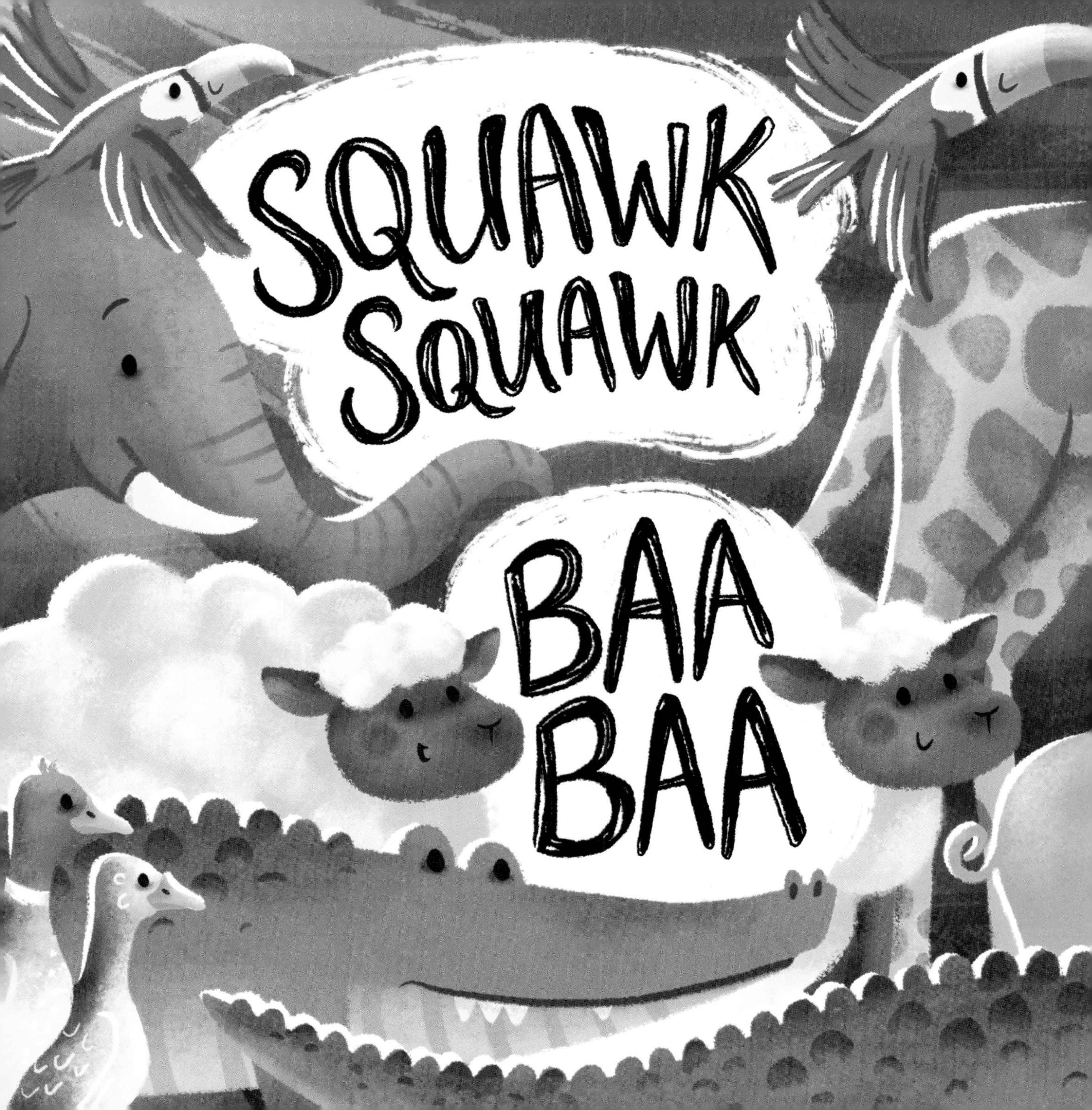
SQUAWK SQUAWK
BAA BAA

Noah and his wife, and their three sons, Shem, Ham, Japheth and their wives...

all went into the ark with the animals.

God shut the door
to keep them all...

SAFE
SAFE
SAFE

just as he
promised.

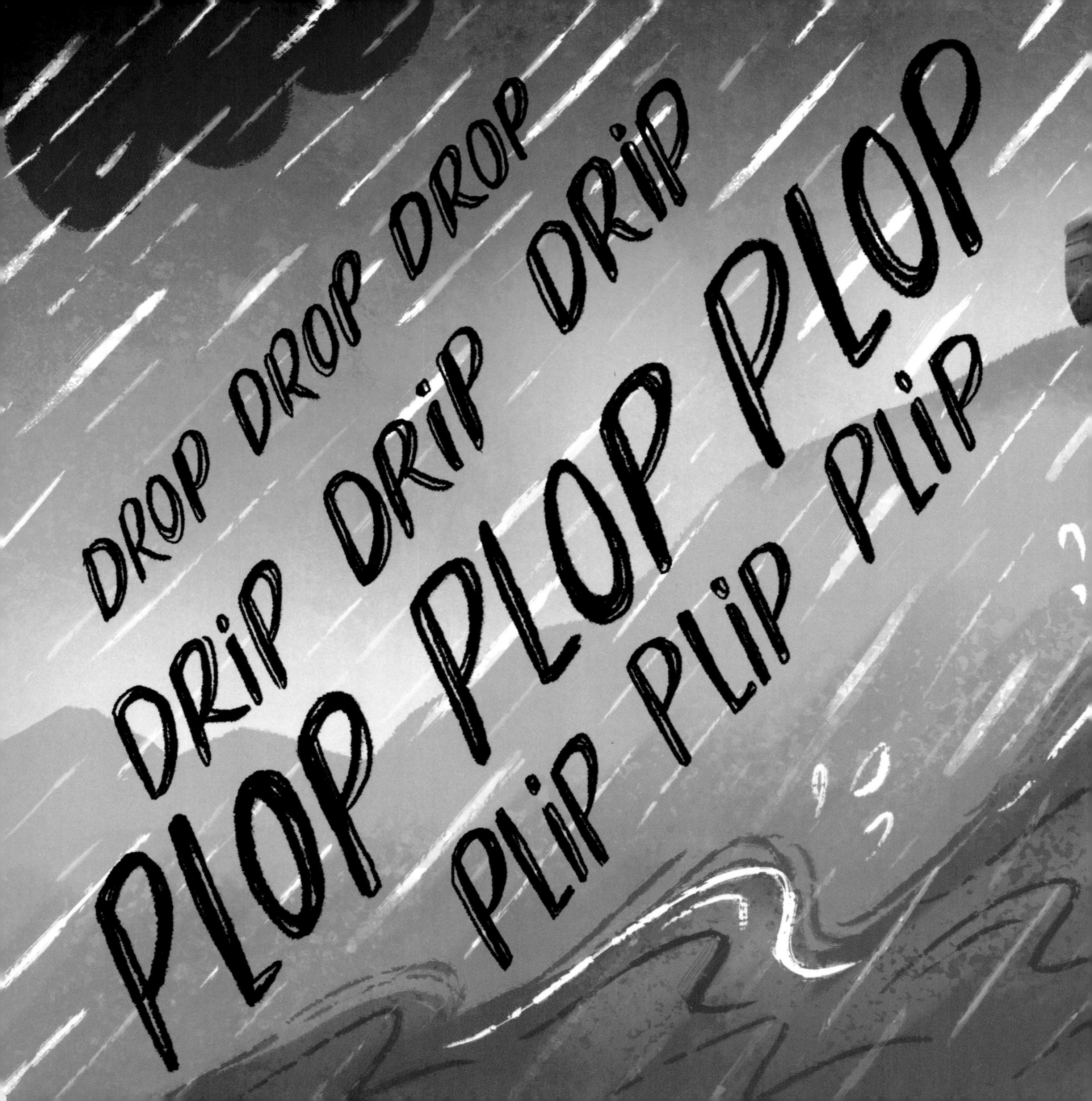
DROP DROP DROP
DRIP DRIP DRIP
PLOP PLOP PLOP
PLIP PLIP PLIP

The rain came down for 40 days and 40 nights, just as God promised.

And the land was flooded so that everything was under water.

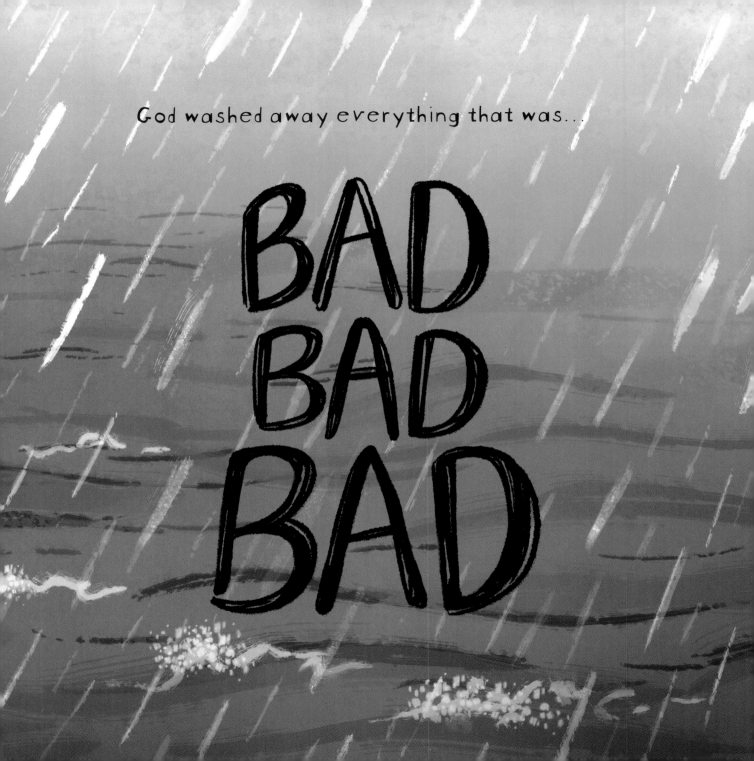

God washed away everything that was...

BAD
BAD
BAD

But Noah and his family were
SAFE SAFE SAFE
in the Very Big Boat
just as God promised.

The water drained slowly away.

GURGLE GURGLE GURGLE GURGLE GLUG GLUG GLUG GLUG

THUMP
BUMP
PLONK

The Very Big Boat came to rest
on Mount Ararat.

Ca-Caw
Ca-Caw
Ca-Caw

Coo Coo Coo

Noah sent out birds to see
if the land was dry again.

When the dove came back with an olive leaf
in its beak, Noah knew the flood had ended.

Noah, his family and all the animals came out of the Very Big Boat into the wonderful washed-clean world that God had given them.

God had kept them all

SAFE SAFE SAFE

just as he promised.

And God made another special promise that day.

"People will still be
BAD BAD BAD.

But **I** promise
I will never again
WASH WASH WASH
them all away."

And God put his bow in the sky to remind everyone of his promise.

So every time you see a rainbow,
remember that God...

ALWAYS
ALWAYS
ALWAYS

keeps his promises.